W9-CNQ-451

Best Thanksgiving Book

ABC Adventures

Written by Pat Whitehead

Illustrated by Susan T. Hall

105.
LIBRARY
ANDERSON ELEMENTARY SCHOOL

Troll Associates

Library of Congress Cataloging in Publication Data

Whitehead, Patricia.
  Best Thanksgiving book.

  (ABC adventures)
  Summary: Retells the story of the first Thanksgiving,
while introducing the reader to the letters of the
alphabet.
  1. Children's stories, American. [1. Thanksgiving—
Fiction. 2. Alphabet] I. Hall, Susan T., ill.
II. Title. III. Series.
PZ7.W5852Bh   1985   [E]   84-8831
ISBN 0-8167-0371-X (lib. bdg.)
ISBN 0-8167-0372-8 (pbk.)

Copyright © 1985 by Troll Associates, Mahwah, New Jersey.
All rights reserved. No part of this book may be used or
reproduced in any manner whatsoever without written permission
from the publisher.
Printed in the United States of America.

10 9 8 7 6 5 4 3 2 1

Do you know the story of the first Thanksgiving?

Aa

America

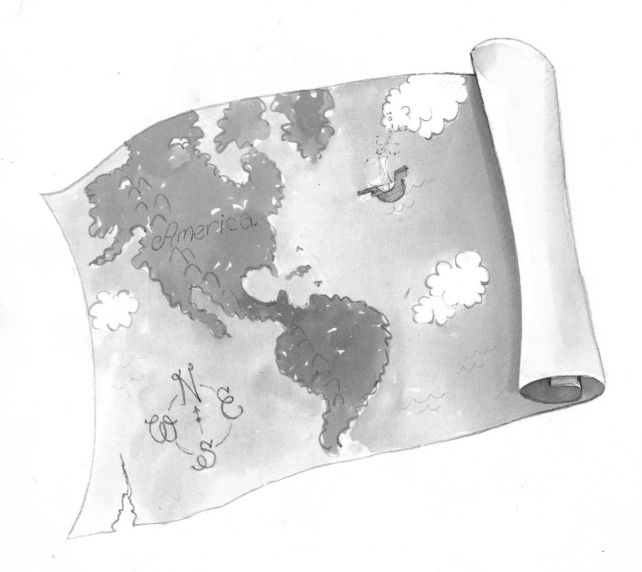

Many years ago, the Pilgrims came to America.

Bb

big

They sailed on a big ship, called the Mayflower.

Cc

courage

It took courage to cross the ocean.

Dd

dangers

There were many dangers.

Ee

eat

When they landed, the Pilgrims
needed food to eat.

Ff

forest

They looked for fresh food in the forest.

Gg

gathered

They gathered seeds and berries to eat.

Hh

hard

The first winter in America was long and hard.

Ii

ill

Many of the Pilgrims became ill.

Jj

joy

When spring finally came, it was a time of joy.

Kk

kind

One day, a kind Indian
came to the Pilgrim's village.

Ll

liked

He liked the Pilgrims and
wanted to help them.

Mm

more

Soon, more Indians came.

Nn

nice

They were nice and showed
the Pilgrims how to plant corn.

Oo

One

One of the Indians was called Squanto.
He was their special friend.

Pp

peace

The Indians and Pilgrims
agreed to live in peace.

Qq

quail

Together they hunted quail and turkey.

Rr

ready

They would be ready for the coming winter.

Ss

summer

When summer ended, the Pilgrims
wanted to have a feast.

Tt

thanks

They had plenty of food and many
new friends. They wanted to give thanks.

Uu

us

"Join us," they said to the Indians.
"Join us in a big feast of thanksgiving."

Vv

very

"It will be a very special holiday."

Ww

wonderful

The Indians came for the feast. Long tables
were filled with wonderful things to eat.

Xx

excited

Everyone was excited.

Yy

yelled

Zz

zigzag

The children yelled and played.
They ran zigzag here and there.

And everyone gave thanks.
What a wonderful Thanksgiving Day.